TERE JOHNSON, MA PS CMF

Dearly Beloved

Launch a Lifetime of Love with Marriage Preparation For Starters

To my beloved Randy

Contents

Chapter 1: Introduction

Dearly beloved, welcome to this starters guide for marriage preparation! You have picked up this book, more than likely because you've made the wonderful, amazing, fantastic decision to get married and very soon, you will be hearing the officiant at your wedding saying these very words at the beginning of your marriage ceremony. Congratulations!

My name is Tere Johnson. I have worked in the field of marriage and family life education for more than a decade and in that time, I have worked with hundreds of couples in your shoes. I have also worked with church ministers, clergy and volunteers who love marriage and serve couples in marriage preparation and marriage enrichment in their churches or organizations. This is literally a labor of love! I decided to write this book because the topic of marriage and marriage education seems to be a secret in our society. While getting married is the most important thing you will ever do, there is an assumption that couples know everything there is to know about getting married and that good marriages just happen. Sadly, neither of these assumptions are true.

Engaged couples don't know what they don't know when it comes to marriage prep! Most have never gone through the process of getting married before. Marriage is a difficult state in life so when couples go into it blindly, it tends to end badly. Married couples who are unable to figure out how to get and stay married keep divorce lawyers in business, and that's all I have to say about that.

This little book is an introduction to the marriage preparation process. You can think of it as a little starter book and guide to the many important things you will want to pay attention to in the year (or months) before your big "I DO". This book does not pretend to be a full blown marriage preparation course. (That will come later my friends). This resource is designed to be a quick read to give you the highlights and best tips and information about how you can get the most out of this precious time before your wedding.

I have worked in the field of marriage education for more than a decade, but I am also married. My husband Randy and I took the big leap into married life more than 30 years ago! I remember the day Randy proposed to me, on a beach on Galveston Island, TX. We were so young! We were both in college and on a trip to Galveston Randy pulled out a little ring, and asked me to marry him. I said "Yes" and then I realized, "Oh shit, we've only been dating for 3 months, what did I just do!" I guess I was caught up in the moment, but a day later, I actually took back my yes. I told Randy I loved him very much, but I felt we were rushing into marriage. While I knew in my heart this was the guy I was going to marry, I felt a bit irresponsible about accepting the proposal after dating him for such a short time.

Being the great guy that he is, Randy was understanding and we continued our relationship, with the marriage proposal always in the background. Finally, after about a year of dating, we took the step to get married. Since I am Catholic, I felt that getting married in the Catholic Church made the best sense, even though, at the time, I didn't appreciate nor cared for my religion that much.

We started our journey at St. John Catholic Church in San Marcos, TX. We saw a priest there who explained the process (about two meetings with him and an engaged couples retreat) and we were on our way. We were married at that church on December 17, 1988. I suppose we are now what some would call a "mature couple". It is really incredible to think back and reminisce. It seems like just yesterday we started on our marriage journey.

You might presently still be in the glow of your epic proposal. Was there skywriting involved, or maybe just a nice dinner with wine and roses? Today, men spend tons of energy and time thinking about the perfect way to propose. As easy or difficult as guys make the proposal, it is truly just the beginning. It's actually the beginning of the beginning, if that makes any sense. Much more is coming your way in the near future as you prepare and I hope you will be as dedicated and devote some time and energy to preparing for your wedding and your marriage.

You should know one thing as you dive into the pages of this book, I am really rooting for you. Most people who work in marriage education, me included, are not in for money or glory! We are involved in this beautiful field because marriage matters. Your marriage matters because it's the foundation of civil society. Without strong marriages and strong families, our world will disintegrate into complete and utter chaos. It is already happening. The lack of marriage has already destroyed many communities. Your marriage is a part of the solution.

In the following pages, you will find some very practical information, but I also hope you will also come to appreciate the importance of learning and the importance of cherishing and respecting your beloved, more every day, from now and for the rest of your life.

Chapter 2: Why Marriage and Why Now?

In my years of working in the marriage education field, I occasionally run into marriage haters that make comments about how marriage is an outdated institution and that there is a major young adult exodus from marriage all across the globe. While there are statistics showing that couples are not getting married at the same rates as they have historically, I argue that the flight from marriage is not really a flight from marriage, it is indeed a flight from what generations of married couples have turned marriage into.

The decades that came after the Sexual Revolution of the 1960's saw the most terrible deformation of the marriage state the world has ever seen. The primary foundational pillars of marriage, which are permanence, faithfulness, and openness to children, turned into "trial marriages", no-fault divorce, a tsunami of pornography, adultery, abuse, and a culture of contraception and abortion that devalues and hates children. So I insist to these naysayers that believe couples don't desire marriage anymore, to just look at the number of couples who enter into pseudo marriages by moving in together and sharing a common domestic life.

No sir, couples are not afraid of marriage, they desire it wholeheartedly, what they hate is what three generations before them turned marriage into, a monster made up of abuse, infidelity, divorce, and brokenness.

Marriage is too important to give up on and I applaud you for taking the step to make the commitment to your beloved. But desiring marriage isn't enough. It is the first step. To enter conscientiously into the married state it is important to know what it is and what it takes to make it work, that is what marriage preparation and education is all about and for the sake of your future marriage and the beautiful children you will bring into the world , I invite you to embrace it fully, with an open mind and an open heart.

So to start... Marriage is a unique relationship, a life-long union between a man and woman that is good for the couple and necessary for the children that will come from that union. It has some universal characteristics that includes permanence, faithfulness, and openness to children. Marriage truly is a beautiful thing that predates the church, the state, and every single institution on planet earth. It is beautiful even if it is difficult at times. You will never regret investing time, and yes, money into building up your relationship and your marriage. Get married with your eyes wide open and with a humble heart, willing to spend a lifetime learning and growing. If you do, you can't go wrong.

Being in the field of marriage education, I am privileged to have relationships and contact with other people who work in this field. One organization I rely on for much of the data I share about marriage in my courses is the Institute for Family Studies, a think tank of marriage educators, counselors, and social scientists who specialize in marriage and family education. You may not realize how important your marriage is, but these folks and I do.

According to IFS research, women and men who get and stay married are healthier, happier, and financially better off, than those who are not married. Married men tend to live about a decade longer than unmarried men. Women are better off financially as retirees when they are married, and communities with larger shares of married couples take care of the poor in their communities. The benefits of marriage to children are impressive. Children who live with their married parents are more likely to finish high school, avoid jail, and avoid teenage pregnancy.

Believe it not, your healthy, lifelong marriage is the best gift you will ever give to your children, and it's the best gift you will give to society. If you are churchgoing, it is the best gift you will give to your faith community.

So why have you chosen marriage?

The reasons engaged couples give for choosing marriage are wide and varied. Some of the reasons are quite disturbing in fact. Have you come to your decision to marry in a thoughtful way? Have you asked the tough questions? Are you sure this is the right person for you? Is this the right time?

These are the million dollar questions, and they demand honest answers, "Why did you decide to get married?" In my work, this is one of the first questions I ask couples and the answers are truly eye opening. Here are a few:

"We've been living together for years so we decided it's time."
  "My grandparents told me they were going to disinherit me."
  "We've been dating for 12 years and everyone thinks we should marry."

"I feel guilty I have been having sex outside of marriage so I want to make

   it right."

   "We're pregnant."

   "We love each other."

   "He (She) makes me happy."

   "My biological clock is ticking."

   "I don't want to be alone."

I came across one case when I worked for a large Catholic archdiocese in Texas some years ago where a maid of honor contacted my office, horrified that the bride had confided in her that the groom was forcing her to marry, under threat of suicide. Clearly, being coerced into marriage by a mentally ill partner is not a good reason to get married, and would be, by the way, an invalid union in the Catholic Church. It is important to recognize the signs of domestic abuse and seek help.

Whether it is undue and unhealthy pressure from family, the fiancee, or feelings of desperation, couples often get married for all the wrong reasons. So it is important to make the decision together, and make the decision after a good period of fully engaged and purposeful dating.

So what is a good and mature reason to take the step into marriage? While it may be slightly different for every couple... the core is this: Are you ready to give your life away to your beloved? Are you ready to make your beloved's needs your own? Are you ready to forgo all others? Would you die for this person? Are you willing to sacrifice your wants and needs for the sake of your beloved?

The wise King Solomon is given credit for the famous lines... "There is a time and a season for everything," this is the season to prepare for your marriage. Prepare well for married life and you will see the fruits of the time and effort you've invested. Marriage is difficult but rewarding. It is naive to believe one can just wing it. There are more challenges threatening marriage today than there have ever been, so couples must work diligently before and during their marriage to fortify their relationship. Use this time to look inward, look deeply and find out what you are made of. You are after all, going to wrap yourself in your finest, and present yourself to another as a gift, that is the truth of marriage.

Photo by Lombe K/Pexels

Chapter 3: Planning For Your Wedding Day

Preparing for the wedding day is the first difficult thing you will do as a couple. Sorting out the responsibilities and deciding who is going to be responsible for what is important. In this chapter, I will discuss some important items to tackle in general, in Chapter Seven, I get into the particularities of religious and non-religious weddings.

First, let me get a little something out of the way. Taking care of wedding details is not just a woman's responsibility. If there is one thing that starts off a marriage on the wrong foot, it is when the bride takes over all the wedding plans and the groom is made to feel excluded. "All I have to do is just show up on the day of the wedding!" joke many of the grooms I have worked with. That just won't do.

Initially, guys may like the idea of their brides taking over the reins of the planning, but in the long run, men end up feeling uninvolved and disconnected. The wedding is the day TWO people pledge their lives to each other and they both are equally responsible for planning it.

Sorry ladies, it's not all about you and what you want. One of the most irritating experiences I've had to endure, back when I used to have a newspaper subscription, was seeing the pictures of all the lovely brides in the wedding announcements section. My visceral reaction to these pictures was usually to yell out.. "WHERE'S THE DAMN GROOM!!!" It takes two to tango when it comes to marriage as you well know, so approaching the wedding planning as a couple is a test of how well you can work together on a big project. There is no bigger project of course than your actual marriage, but wedding planning is a good place to start.

Wedding Planning Guides

While I don't have any particular wedding planning guide to recommend, the important tip here is simply to use one. There are many on the market that help couples think through all the different aspects of wedding planning. If you are thrifty and can get by with a simple one, you can use the one I created and included in the back of this book.

To begin your wedding planning make sure you put first things first. If you are churchgoing and belong to a particular religious tradition, go to your church or congregation FIRST. Don't make any big decisions about venues or catering or photography before checking in with your faith community. One of the most common fires I had to put out during my time working for a large archdiocese in Texas, were the flames created when couples put down large deposits on reception halls and caterers, and then found out their church was not available on the day they picked. This caused fireworks between clergy, parish staff and the couples. In one corner, you had the couples demanding their day, and on the other, you had church staff insisting they were booked.

While your wedding is very special, keep in mind there are *other* couples getting married and churches may have other events already scheduled. Try to avoid "cart before the horse" thinking and decision making. Don't blame the church for your decision to put the cart (venue) before the horse (church) When these situations happen, couples end up having to go church hunting. Can you say unnecessary stress? While the reception venue is very important, it is not more important than your church or temple. Don't make any decisions or drop serious $$$ bucks on ANYTHING before you talk to someone at your church. Different faith communities handle marriages in their own unique ways. More on that in the final chapter.

If you are not religious or belong to a religious community, check in with the courthouse to find the process of getting married there or for hiring a justice of the peace to officiate at your chosen wedding venue.

Back to wedding planning guides. If you choose to invest in a comprehensive wedding planning guide, look for journal style wedding guides that include the entire wedding planning process, from A-Z with lots of room to write and check-lists. Be aware that many wedding planning guides do not address the need to contact your Church, Congregation, or courthouse first, which is leads couples down the wrong track. Just think about it, these are the places where *your actual* ceremony will take place or will be providing your officiant, so they must come first.

Wedding Websites

Another good resource you can look into are wedding planning websites. Wedding planning websites typically have a wealth of information and some provide ways to create your wedding registry. Be aware that many wedding planning websites sell ads for companies in the wedding industry that may or may not be legitimate. Do your research on any company you choose to become involved with. When hiring companies, support your local shops and service providers as much as possible.

If you haven't discovered them yet, the Knot.com have excellent resources as does Wedding Wire.com.

Wedding Planners

A quick word on wedding planners. If you have a large budget and your wedding involves many moving parts, like a destination wedding, it is good to utilize the expertise of a wedding planning professional. Make sure you conduct a thorough interview and check references before hiring a wedding planner. Be aware that some faith communities (Catholic) do not work with wedding planners. The reason for this is that religious celebrations include many rites and rituals most wedding planners are unfamiliar with. Wedding planners end up venturing into sacred territory they don't know anything about. If you are Catholic and you want to use a wedding planner, just ensure that they stay in their lane. They can help with everything except the religious ceremony. Catholic churches normally have wedding coordinators that assist with the rehearsal and during the ceremony.

When it comes to any aspect of your wedding, ask lots of questions and if your gut is telling you there is something wrong, chances are you are right. There are scammers galore in the wedding industry, just looking for their next target.

Wedding planners who work with agencies are also the best resource if you are interested in a destination wedding. Interview any potential companies you think may be able to assist you with a destination wedding.

One final thing on destination weddings, if you are planning a religious wedding at your destination, make sure you have someone locally helping you prepare all the necessary paperwork that is required. In the Catholic Church, couples have to do all of their marriage preparation in their home church or diocese and special paperwork must be completed by the diocese for marriage files to be transferred to overseas dioceses for destination weddings.

Tips for DIY Weddings on a Budget

If you have a small budget for your wedding, don't sweat it. You can have a beautiful wedding without breaking the bank. The key is, keep it very simple, and keep the guest list short. Create a budget and stick to it. There are many things you can do to save money.

Here are some examples: Purchase your flowers and wedding cake from a grocer. Buy your wedding dress off the rack or visit a vintage shop and recycle someone's old wedding dress. Some would say otherwise, but you CAN find a beautiful wedding dress for less than $1,000.00. If you know where to look, you can even find some beautiful gowns for less than $500.00. If you can avoid it, do not purchase wedding dresses from unknown online sellers. There have been nightmarish stories about dresses ordered online that upon arriving look NOTHING like the pictures on the internet.

In Mexico, where I'm from, there is a beautiful tradition of "padrinos" or sponsors who help pay for different parts of a wedding. Whether or not you are Mexican, you can talk to family and friends and ask them if they may be able to help you with certain things you need, in lieu of wedding gifts. You can create a special fund your loved ones can contribute to, to pay for catering, photography, or your honeymoon. Mexico was into crowdfunding way before it was a thing! Who knew!

Many things that are commonly outsourced can be done very nicely at home. Programs for the religious ceremony can be done at home, as well as wedding favors. For her wedding, our daughter Phoebe created labels for Mint LifeSavers that said "Phoebe and Patrick : Mint to Be" . They were a big hit at the reception. Patrick's family took care of making centerpieces for the tables at the reception. There are many ideas floating around on the internet for DIY weddings.

One of the saddest things I ever heard when working with older couples who have lived together for decades and finally decided to get married was that they were waiting to have money to have a big reception. There again, is cart before the horse thinking. If you don't have money for a big party, and you want to get married, GET MARRIED! Go to a nice restaurant for dinner and call it a day. Getting married is the important part, everything else is just icing on the cake.

Wedding Attire

A wedding coordinator I know tells the story of a wedding in which she was assisting, where the bride shocked the guests with her dress. She says she was mortified when the bride walked out of the brides' room wearing a dress that while beautiful and fully covered on the front, was totally backless. The back was cut so low, you could actually see her butt crack. So, family and guests were treated to "crack" during her very long walk to the altar. The wedding coordinator said that as long as the bride didn't turn around, she would not moon the clergy. She recalls, "I kept praying, don't turn around, don't turn around, don't turn around!" The priest who was officiating was very strict about modesty and seeing the bride's crack would have certainly sent him over the edge, "If we got through the entire ceremony without her turning around, we would be OK," she said. That's what happened. When she finally turned around, the ceremony was over and that was that.

I was asked by one family to intervene in a case where a wedding coordinator at a church had seen a picture of the bride in her dress and respectfully asked her to make sure she brought a shawl or a bolero to the church ceremony. The dress was strapless and extremely revealing. When I spoke to the bride's mother, she said her daughter was devastated that her beautiful designer dress would have to be covered up. "It's the dress of her dreams." The situation got so heated the family was threatening to cancel the wedding and leave the Catholic Church! I talked with the family over a couple of days to try to diffuse the situation. It seemed to me that the dress had become the center of attention with the actual marriage ceremony being left in the dust. After several conversations with the mom and the bride, in which I tried to explain the sacredness of the ceremony and the need for modesty, they opted to cover up, under protest of course.

It is interesting that we rarely have any problems with men's apparel! That must be because men's attire is almost always very modest. Something has certainly happened to women's fashion in general and wedding gowns in particular. It's disturbing to me as a woman and a mom, that fabric is missing from some very interesting parts of dresses! Mostly the top, but sometimes also the sides, the back, the length, etc. While I understand some women prefer revealing clothing, a wedding is not the place for it. It is very distracting. Beauty and class should be the order of the day. Clothing should enhance and provide proper coverage so as to not lead the eye to focus on any particular part of the body. Do this for yourself and do it for your guests, who really don't want to see your breasts coming out of your dress. Well, some might, but if they do, they're creepers who shouldn't be at your wedding!

Modesty should be the order of the day for everyone, for the bride's gown, the bride's maids dresses, the men's formals, as well as the parents of the bride and groom. As I always told my daughters when dress shopping... "say no to crack, in the front and in the back." Yes, mom jokes are as bad as dad jokes!

Marriage License

Speaking of in-laws, do you think your future in-laws might be a little nosy? They are nothing compared to the government which is involved in every little thing in our lives, including marriage. To make your marriage valid and legal in the eyes of the state you have to get either a marriage license or in some countries, like in Mexico, couples have to get married civilly first and the religious wedding is viewed by the state as simply ceremonial.

In the United States, church ministers have faculties to officiate at weddings, so couples simply have to get their marriage license and take it to the minister officiating at the wedding for him or her to execute it. This doesn't mean the minister takes the marriage license behind the shed and shoots it, it means the minister signs it and returns it to the government office that issued it. Usually that's the county clerk's office where you originally obtained it.

Look into the requirements for obtaining a marriage license and when it can be executed in your particular state. In the State of Texas, for instance, couples can get a marriage license as early as three months before the wedding, and as late as 3 days before. The rules vary state by state, so it is important to find out what the rules are in your particular jurisdiction. Regardless, don't forget your wedding has a civil aspect to it that needs to be taken into consideration.

Photo by Jonathan Borba/Pexels

Chapter 3: Planning For Your Wedding Day

Chapter 4: Planning For Married Life

As incredibly important planning for your wedding DAY is, you are truly planning for one, maybe two days worth of activities that will carry you and your fiance over the threshold from singlehood into married life. When you wake up the next day after your wedding, you are no longer single Mary and single William, you are a brand new married couple. So what can you do to strengthen your marriage bond before you get married? That's called marriage preparation, or marriage education.

You might be asking yourself, why do I even need anything like this, isn't love all we need to make it work? Well, love is of primary importance, but you also need many skills to navigate married life. All the love in your heart means nothing, if you don't know how to express it, and that's a skill.

What to Look For

There are many great marriage education books and courses on the market. Some of my favorites include FOCCUS, Prepare-Enrich, and

SYMBIS (Saving your Marriage Before it Starts). These are considered relationship assessments that are used with trained facilitators, marriage coaches, or counselors. There are also many faith based and standard programs designed for teams of marriage educators to present as weekend retreats or class series.

There are different areas or topics that are vital for engaged couples to explore with each other before they get married, which the programs mentioned above are supposed to do. In the many years I have been reviewing programs, no one program touches on 100% of the important topics in marriage. The topics include, self awareness, marriage readiness, family of origin, communication, conflict management, financial styles and management, personalities, views on commitment, intimacy, sex and children, mixed religion or faith issues and spirituality.

Christian faith based programs I have worked with and worked on for many years go further and help couples explore the theology of marriage, the importance of covenant, a couple's relationship with God and the church, living the virtues in marriage, and family values including openness to children.

If your new marriage is a second one for either of you, seek out specialized programs for couples entering into a remarriage, especially if there are children from previous marriages or relationships. Remarriage ministry is relatively new in the Catholic Church, I've worked with a wonderful team for many years who put on the New Life Retreat in my home diocese. This program was specifically created with remarriage in mind and has expanded beyond our area. Ron Deal created the *Smart Stepfamily* program and has become one of the leaders in remarriage education in the United States.

The Dreaded Elephant in the Room

In the marriage education world there is an elephant in the room. There are very well meaning folks putting out books and programs about marriage with solid content, but *it's what's missing* that's alarming. Many authors and program creators are afraid of how addressing this elephant is going to make you feel and avoid it like the plague.

I address the elephant in the room because I care about you and your future marriage too much to withhold important information. Depending on where you are in your relationship journey, this information could make a difference in your marriage. What is this elephant? The elephant is *cohabitation* - living as husband and wife **without** marriage. Living together seems to be the go to living situation when a couple decides to take things to another level, and often it is done with very good intentions. Besides it seeming like the logical next step, couples often move in together for financial reasons, but cohabitation has turned out to be disastrous for many reasons.

Social scientists have been studying the effects of cohabitation on marriage for decades. One renowned researcher who has done extensive work in this area is Dr. Scott Stanley from the University of Denver. According to his research, living together or cohabitation continues to be linked to poor outcomes in marriage.

Some of the major issues plaguing couples who live together are mentioned by Dr. Stanley and colleagues include couples drifting into marriage without ever conscientiously choosing it. Dr. Stanley says couples who live together tend to stay together longer when serious problems arise, when living apart would have led to a swift break-up. This is complicated further when these couples have children, and then the children end up becoming another reason stick it out, even if the relationship lacks commitment and is of very low quality. In these cases, when there is finally a break-up, these couples find it difficult to navigate new relationships with children in tow.

Many marriage educators have given up on talking about this topic because it has become such an overwhelming cultural phenomenon. Just take a look at these statistics on living together without marriage from the Census Bureau:

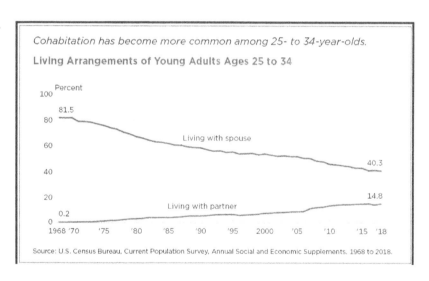

Cohabitation has become more common among 25- to 34-year-olds.
Living Arrangements of Young Adults Ages 25 to 34

In the late 1960's 81.5% of young adults between the ages of 25-34 were married and a tiny fraction .2% were living together. The number of married people in the same age bracket who were married plummeted to 40.3% by 2018. In 2018 the number of young adults who were living together increased by 146% to 14.8 %, and the number continues to rise.

With numbers like these, you would think they were giving away free puppies with every move in and relationship quality would be out of this world, but the contrary has turned out to be true, as illustrated by Dr. Scott Stanley's research.

Among 18-24 year olds, the percentage of couples living together without marriage has overtaken the number of married couples in that age bracket. There are now more couples living together without marriage in this age group than there are married couples.

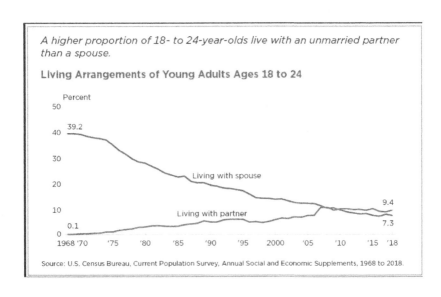

A higher proportion of 18- to 24-year-olds live with an unmarried partner than a spouse.

Living Arrangements of Young Adults Ages 18 to 24

Source: U.S. Census Bureau, Current Population Survey, Annual Social and Economic Supplements, 1968 to 2018.

You would think that the popularity of cohabitation for more than 50 years now would translate into rock solid marriages, but the reality is that living together is not good marriage preparation, in fact, the opposite is true. As it turns out, living together leads to marriage only 50% of the time and those couples who do end up married report lower levels of marital satisfaction after one year of marriage.

You might be thinking, well, that train left the station, we've lived together and are now preparing to marry. If this is your situation, I share this data with you simply because you should know that if you have lived together more than one year, you will have to be very watchful for signs of marital drift and make a special effort to focus on commitment. Commitment is crucial to marriage, and living together is actually the antithesis of commitment. Why? The premise of moving in together is to test things out and if things don't work out, then, there's the door. This is nothing like a marriage commitment when you declare to each other and the world... dearly beloved, there is no door.

I don't share this information to alarm you if you have lived with your future spouse. I share this information to make you aware that you will have to be extra vigilant and more deliberate about your marriage, than couples who have not lived together as husband and wife, before saying "I DO."

Saving the living together and sex part for married life, isn't just for those who are religiously minded. Cohabitation and sex before marriage have been proven to be detrimental for couples who choose it, regardless of religious beliefs. If something is poison, it doesn't matter who drinks it, it will kill indiscriminately. Couples don't have to move-in together to "test" the relationship. That's what marriage education is for.

Photo by SDI Productions / iStock

Chapter 5: Planning Your Family

Having children is one of the greatest joys my husband Randy and I have ever experienced. We waited four years before ordering our first, and had a total of four daughters over the next 16 years of marriage. We recently became first time grandparents and we are overjoyed at seeing our family grow.

Children are a blessing, and our ability to create life and bring children into the world with our spouse is truly a gift. Do you sense that the world sees our ability to have children as a gift? The answer to that question is a resounding NO. Babies, the precious fruit of human love, are seen as an inconvenience and as an obstacle to personal fulfillment and success. It's really a sad state of affairs (pardon the pun). There seems to be a full, all out war against the human body, our fertility and precious newborn life. There are people who have made it their life's work to dehumanize and destroy our ability to have children. Something evil is afoot! While I do get my cues about the innate dignity of men and women from my faith, you don't have to be religious to appreciate the beauty of the human body and our ability to have children. There is something powerful and strong about a man's ability to be a father; and likewise, there is something beautiful and nurturing about a woman's ability to be a mother. Our ability to have children is not a disease, but it is treated as if it were one by certain people.

From doctors, to corporations, to some churches, maternity continues to be viewed in American culture as undesirable. Now sex, that's a different story. Our media, movies, tv shows and magazines can't give consumers enough of it. Sterile, meaningless sex. There is an entire industrial complex that has as adopted a philosophy and has made a mission out of promoting the idea that sex is only for pleasure. The natural connection between sex and babies and also the connection between marriage and sex has all but disappeared to our own demise.

Waving the banner of women's rights, some groups have adopted an unreal and cruel vision of human sexuality that is truly inhuman. It is inhuman because it seeks to remove or neutralize those things that make us truly men and women, and turns us into some kind of idiot sex robots. This philosophy is contrary to how we are made as human beings. So while advances in women's health in the areas that really matter, such as heart disease (the #1 killer of women), cancer and strokes, has stagnated, the medical and pharmaceutical community thinks one more contraceptive pill, patch, ring, or IUD, is the answer to all of our female health problems.

So back to family planning. So if most of what we see in our culture is harmful to women and the marriage relationship by extension, what is real family planning? How can we approach it in a way that doesn't diminish our natural state of being? Real family planning sees fertility as a natural part of the human condition, not as a disease that must be vanquished. Crush, kill, destroy those ovaries! Tie the tubes, rip out the womb, snip, snip, snip that vasa deferentia (aka vasectomy). Real family planning follows the hippocratic oath that physicians should do no harm to men or women.

The only family planning methods that respect womens overall health and their delicate reproductive system, as well as men's health and wellbeing is Natural Family Planning. There are different types of natural family planning methods that are designed to give couples more or less information they can use to keep track of their fertility and have sex whenever they want if they want to get pregnant, or simply abstain from sex on the days when sexual activity is more likely to produce a baby. Modern methods of Natural Family Planning are well researched and scientifically based. Some of my favorites include the Partnership Method, the Couple to Couple League, Creighton Model Fertility Care, Billings, and the Marquette Method.

Natural Family Planning does not interfere, in any way, with a woman's hormones so there are no side effects, except for good ones, the primary one being great communication about family planning between husband and wife!

When Randy and I first got married, we were totally in the dark about Natural Family Planning, so we used the birth control pill. It always felt like I had to take care of this aspect of our relationship and I really came to resent it. I resented this, especially because all the different birth control pills my doctor prescribed, made me very sick. All my doctor did was prescribe me a different one each time I complained about it. This began to take a toll on my health and our relationship. After about 4 years of struggling with birth control we decided to stop the pill-insanity and try for a baby.

It took us about a year to conceive. Not at all happy with the pill we tried other methods of contraception in those years following our first baby. I didn't know it right away, but the hormones and chemicals in the products I was using resulted in painful cysts on my ovaries that required two surgeries to remove. After those painful experiences and after learning about what my faith taught about these harmful contraceptives, I proposed to Randy we try Natural Family Planning. Natural Family Planning involves both the husband and the wife in the monitoring of fertility, so it just seemed right. My resentment about having to deal with the family planning aspect of our relationship and nagging emotions about feeling used, began to melt away. My body and our relationship began to heal.

While some people may insist on it, Natural Family Planning is not just for Catholics. While the Catholic Church supports natural methods that respect the human body, Protestants and non-religious couples have also gravitated toward Natural Family Planning for different reasons. Some couples are extremely health conscious and don't want to introduce hormones of any kind into their bodies. Other couples learn NFP because they want to have a baby and heard that charting is a good way to determine the most fertile times, others are looking to space the births of their children in a way that makes financial sense to them, while others like the idea of 100% natural unadulterated sex. Natural Family Planning or NFP also helps couples become so close, some have even called it marriage insurance.

You might be asking yourself when is a good time to learn NFP. Most methods take several months to learn, so starting a course 6-9 months before your wedding is a good time frame.

Chapter 6: Planning For Tough Times

It may seem very difficult to imagine it right now, while you are both so in love and floating on cloud 9, to think about the times when the ship is going to hit the fan. If there is something you can be sure of, it's that you will have tough times in your marriage. In marriage education, we call this the marriage roller coaster or the natural cycles of marriage.

In marriage you will experience times of excitement and joy, you will experience confusion and bewilderment, you will experience frustration and disillusionment, you will experience deep pain and loss. That is the nature of marriage. It's not all roses. The key to a lifelong marriage is to be so committed to your beloved that you will always find a way to forgive and stay. The work you put in learning about each other, and learning about ways to strengthen your relationship will pay off here. A couple who is building a strong marriage, will not be torn asunder when the storms come. That is why marriage educators insist on getting couples started on the right foot, but then recommend couples continue doing things together so they never experience marital drift.

So what will you do if you experience something you feel like you cannot overcome as a couple? The first thing I will say is… don't go to your parents. Family involvement in marital problems causes distancing between the parties. Your mother will never see your husband again in the same light, if you tell her about the problems you are having with him. If you're the guy and you go and tell your mother about the problems you are having with your wife, she will never see her the same way ever again. Don't do that to your family.

When you hit the brick wall with a conflict or problem you can't resolve, go to a marriage coach or a professional counselor. Marriage coaches can offer basic relationship skills and will refer you to professional counseling if you need extra help. Marriage coaches are also more budget friendly. If you don't find a marriage coach at your church, or in your community, go directly to professional counseling, not not pass go, go directly to therapy. Don't see your decision to go to counseling as a failure. You are doing yourself and your marriage a great favor by seeking out help. Look for a marriage friendly therapist who will do everything in his power to help you heal the hurts and get back on track.

I remember being in tears, the first time I called my church for a counseling referral when Randy and I were locking horns. I felt like we had failed somehow but my pride was not more important than our marriage. Seeking help is not a weakness, it is a strength. Couples counseling is a step in the right direction to get you unstuck from whatever issue you are having.

Create a crisis plan now, write it down and put it somewhere safe so that you will remember it when the skies go gray and you are feeling like love is running out. Don't hesitate to get help, the love is there, just around the corner, even if it doesn't look the way it did when you were first dating. Love has to grow and mature, and you will love each other and your marriage more, on the other side of surviving major trouble.

If you are however, in an abusive relationship, and you fear for your safety all bets are off. Your safety always comes first. If you are in an abusive relationship, contact the National Domestic Abuse Hotline at 1-800-799-7233.

Photo by Timur Weber / Pexels

Chapter 7: Religious & Non-Religious Weddings

Christians

Since I have spent most of my marriage education career in the faith based community, I thought I would devote this little section of the book to speak directly to Christian couples who are preparing to marry. While my work has been mostly in the Catholic arena, much of what I will share in these next few paragraphs applies to all couples who wish to have Jesus Christ in the center of their life and their marriage.

If you are a sincere Christian, and I have no doubts that you are, you will agree that the hand of God and the Holy Spirit has seen to it that you and your fiance found each other. Marriage is a God thing, so it is my view that everything that leads us to marriage is gently moved by divine providence.

If you are a Protestant Christian, seek out someone in your faith community and begin the conversation about Christian marriage.

There is a difference between getting married at your church, and simply getting married at the courthouse or at a wedding venue. Houses of worship are sacred places set aside for God, where we gather as a community of believers. It is where we are baptized, where we hear God's word, and are instructed in the ways of the Christian life. The Church is the good and proper place for you to begin your marriage journey. Speak to your pastor, or if you're lucky to have one... your Marriage and Family Pastor to find out what kind of marriage preparation your church offers and get things rolling for your church wedding. If your church doesn't offer any marriage prep, work with your clergy to explore resources in your area. Perhaps a neighboring church offers a program you can join.

If you have just become engaged and you are a baptized Catholic (even non-practicing) connect or reconnect with your Catholic Church. As a baptized Catholic the true and proper place for you to get married is the Catholic Church. Please do not allow shiny objects (like beautiful venues) to distract you from what you truly want or need as a Catholic Christian... a marriage in the Lord in the Catholic Church. Very soon you and your dearly beloved will be one, and will be forming a new family. Now is the time to make the commitment to make your faith a priority and return to Church if you have been away. If you are a practicing Catholic make recommit to the goodness of your Catholic religion and get married in a Catholic Church.

You might be waffling at the idea of marriage in the Catholic Church because of all the ugliness and scandal the Catholic Church has been embroiled in, in the last 30 years. I hear you. There have been things that have happened to me personally, that have affected my trust and faith in Church leadership. There is no doubt there are very problematic people in the Church, but there also is my Lord. A long time ago, I fixed an idea in my heart and my head… I would never give up Jesus and my beautiful ancient Catholic religion, because of the sinful men and women who have defaced her. I remain in the Catholic Church and firmly so because this is where I encounter Jesus, in the Holy Eucharist, in the Confessional, in the Word of God, and in my everyday prayer. I heard someone once ask… "Would you abandon Jesus for the sake of Judas (the traitor)" My answer is no. Do not give up your Catholic religion on the count of the sins of the ones who have betrayed the Church. The Church is a microcosm of the world where saints and sinners are friends.

Non-Christian Religions

If your faith community falls under one of the major non-Christian religions in the world, such as the Jewish tradition, or Buddhist, your religions also honor the married state and have very beautiful wedding ceremonies with many symbolic rituals.

I recently became familiar with some beautiful Jewish traditions. From morning until evening, there are beautiful parts to a Jewish wedding, like the grooms ritual bath (the mikvah), the reading of the Psalms (the tefilah), the beautiful marriage promises (ketubah) and the Chuppah, or the canopy where the couple stands during the ceremony which symbolizes their future home.

Connecting with your roots and participating in wedding ceremonies infused with religious and cultural meaning will get your marriage started off on the right track. If your religious tradition does not include any formal marriage preparation, talk to your religious leaders to find out if standard marriage prep, that focuses on skills and is not sectarian, would be permissible for you.

Non-religious weddings

Many beautiful couples fit in this category. You would think that a non-religious ceremony is simpler, and in some ways it is. But in other ways, it is more complex. For instance, in most churches, there is already a script (in the Catholic Church it is called the Rite of Matrimony) that already includes all of the important parts of the wedding ceremony. In your case, if you want your ceremony to be extra special, you will want to talk to the judge or justice of the peace to find out what is in your ceremony and ask if you can add to it or create your own for it to signify your marriage promises.

If you don't want to get married in the courthouse, you will have to look into wedding venues. If you do get married at a venue, you will have to hire a justice of the peace or freelance minister with faculties to officiate at weddings.

If you are on a budget, don't forget community centers and parks often have very lovely rooms and halls where you can have your ceremony and your reception. For the most part, all the planning is the same, except the location of your ceremony will be different than for those having religious weddings.

Photo by Anderson Santo / Pexels

Chapter 8: Conclusion

A hopeful future and a REAL marriage, imperfect as it will be

Dearly beloved, we have come to the end of this little book. I hope the information here will help you enter into this period of formal engagement with the information you need to make good decisions. Remember, your relationship is unique and your marriage matters very much, to me, as someone who loves my own marriage and the institution of marriage, and to the world, which desperately needs your energy and your joy as a married couple.

Remember to take time and truly reflect on your reasons for choosing marriage, let them be good reasons. Tap in to the many resources that are available to you to help you organize your wedding, and work together. More and more, you will become a team, and the wedding planning process is a great place to start. Truly engage and embrace all the marriage preparation opportunities you come across. Pre-marriage education is designed to help you start off on the right foot and with your eyes wide open. I hope you come to see your own beautiful human nature and your ability to have children as a blessing, because it is! There are natural alternatives to spacing the birth of children that respect your body. Know that there are people who are rooting for you and when things get difficult there is help. A caring marriage coach or counselor is just a phone call away.

Marriage is about to make a comeback, and you are going to be a part of it.

Photo by Rene Asmunsen / Pexels

Resources

Centers for Disease Control and Prevention. (n.d.). *Leading Causes of Death in Females.* Https://Www.Cdc.Gov/Women/Lcod/2018/All-Races-Origins/Index.Htm. Retrieved July 28, 2022, from https://www.cdc.gov/women/lcod/2018/all-races-origins/index.htm

Cherlin, A. J. (2009). The Marriage-Go-Round: The State of Marriage and the Family in America Today. In *The Marriage Go Round: The State of Marriage and Family in America Today* (pp. 17–18). Borzoi / Alfred A. Knopf.

Curtin, S. C., Sutton, P. S., & Centers for Disease Control and Prevention. (2020, April 1). *Marriage Rates in the United States 1900–2018.* Https://Www.Cdc.Gov/Nchs/Data/Hestat/Marriage_rate_2018/Marriage_rate_2018.Htm#suggested. Retrieved July 26, 2022, from https://www.cdc.gov/nchs/data/hestat/marriage_rate_2018/marriage_rate_2018.htm

Ezra, B. E. (2014, September 19). *Jewish wedding traditions explained.* Https://Www.Smashingtheglass.Com/. Retrieved July 28, 2022, from

https://www.smashingtheglass.com/jewish-wedding-traditions-explai
ned/

Gurrentz, B. G. (2018, November 15). *Living with an Unmarried Partner Now Common for Young Adults.* Https://Www.Census.Gov/En.Html. Retrieved July 27, 2022, from https://www.census.gov/library/stories/ 2018/11/cohabitation-is-up-marriage-is-down-for-young-adults.htm l

Institute for Family Studies. (2015, January). *Marriage: Much More Than a Piece of Paper Especially for Children.*

Stanley, S. S. (2018, July 14). *Sliding vs Deciding.* Https://Slidingvsde ciding.Blogspot.Com/2018/07/Cohabitation-Is-Common-Update-on Trends.Html. Retrieved July 27, 2022, from https://slidingvsdeciding.b logspot.com/2018/07/cohabitation-is-common-update-on-trends.ht ml

Checklist for Religious Weddings

___ Contact your church/ congregation/ temple

___ Meet your clergy or minister to get requirements and process for marriage there.

___ Gather important documents required by your church, congregation or temple

___ Select a primary marriage education course

___ Register for your primary marriage education course

___ Finalize your ceremony date/time/place: _____
_____

___ Confirm the name of the church minister officiating:
_____

___ Confirm names of Best Man and Maid of Honor

_____

___ Finalize your reception date/time/location:

_____

___ Register for your natural family planning course:
(Date, time(s), location) _____

_____

___ Register for any supplemental courses needed (Ex.
Finances):_____

___ Attend your primary marriage education course (check
off when completed)

___ Attend your natural family planning course (check off
when completed)

___ Schedule a marriage ceremony planning meeting with
clergy (Ex. Nuptial Mass prep, church ceremony prep,
preparation of the Ketubah and Chuppah)

___ Schedule the wedding rehearsal:(Date/time/location)

_____

___ (Optional) Religious destination wedding? Ask clergy or
ministers about additional paperwork requirements for
marriages outside of your local area. Catholics completed
marriage file must be reviewed and signed off on, by
your local bishop's office before being sent to the
diocese of your destination wedding.

___ (Optional) Religious destination wedding? Contact the embassy of the country you want to travel for state mandated marriage requirements.

___ Get your Marriage License from the county clerk's office in your county.

___ Follow up with clergy a week after the wedding to make sure marriage license was promptly returned to the county office where it originated.

Checklist for Non-Religious Weddings

__ Contact the civil courthouse to gather information about
about your plans to marry (Date/time/place)

_____

Your contacts name & number _____

__ Gather important documents required by the state
needed to obtain your marriage license

__ If you are getting married at a venue contact your top
three favorites for quotes.

__ Select a primary marriage education course:_____

__ Register for your primary marriage education course:
(Date/time/place) _____

__ Finalize your ceremony (date/time/place: _____

_____

__ Confirm the name of the judge or justice of the peace who will be officiating your wedding

__ Confirm names of Best Man and Maid of Honor
These are your two official witness _____
_____

__ Finalize your reception venue (date/times/location)
_____

__ Register for your natural family planning course:
(Date, time(s), location) _____
_____

__ Register for any supplemental courses needed (Ex. Finances):_____

__ Attend your primary marriage education course (check off when completed)

__ Attend your natural family planning course (check off when completed)

__ Get your Marriage License from the county clerk's office in your county.

Wedding Checklist

Wedding Check-list with Expense Tracker

✓	Item	Cost	✓	Item	Cost	✓	Item	Cost
	Save the Date Postcard			Transportation			Reception Hall/ Venue	
	Engagement Photos			Church/Temple Wedding Venue Fees			Rentals Tables/Chairs Other items	
	Engagement Party			Rental Fees Arches/ Deco			Table linens & Centerpieces	
	Wedding Gown			Program Worship Aid			Catering Food / Bev	
	Wedding Veil			Church flowers			Wedding Cake Groom's Cake	
	Shoes			Wedding party flowers			Cake Cutting Cutlery	
	Her Accessories			Musicians / singer stipends			Wine	
	His suit / tuxedo			Stipends for officiant /court fee			Wine Glasses	
	His shoes			Ceremony Photography			Music DJ / Band	
	His Accessories			Pre-wedding activities or meals			Wedding favors	
	Bridal Shower Invitations			Her Wedding Ring			Departing outfits	
	Bridal Shower Invite postage			His Wedding Ring			Thank You's	
	Bridal Shower			Religious Specific			Postage	
	Clothing alterations			Religious Specific			Honeymoon Travel	

For Before the Wedding | **Wedding Ceremony** | **For the Reception & After**

Wedding Checklist 2

Wedding Check-list with Expense Tracker (2)

<u>For Before the Wedding</u>   <u>Our Wedding Ceremony</u>   <u>For the Reception & After</u>

✓	Item	Cost	✓	Item	Cost	✓	Item	Cost
	Wedding Invitations			Religious Specific			Honeymoon Lodging	
	Wedding Invite Postage			Other			Honeymoon Meals	
	Hair & Makeup			Other			Honeymoon Sightseeing	
	Rehearsal Dinner			Other			Passports	
	Wedding Party Gifts (Women)			Other			Luggage	
	Wedding Party Gift (Men)			Other			Spending Money	
	Total Pre-Wedding			Total Ceremony			Total Reception	

(From Dearly Beloved: Launch a Lifetime of Love with Marriage Preparation by Tere Johnson, MA PS, CMF. © 2022)

Printable Checklists

Dearly beloved... printable PDF files of the checklists included in this book are available by contacting Bonaventure Publishing at the following e-mail address! Request yours today!

BonaventurePublishing@outlook.com

About the Author

Teresita (Tere) Johnson, MA PS, CMF, is an experienced marriage education specialist who has worked in the faith based marriage preparation community for 12 years. Tere has worked with hundreds of engaged and married couples and has shared her knowledge about different marriage education programs and tools, training hundreds of couples and clergy to help new marriages get off on the right foot, and strengthen already married ones. She is presently President of Stella Maris Center, a nonprofit organization based in League City, TX, whose mission is to strengthen marriage and family life. She lives in League City, TX with her husband Randy and the last of their four children, Trinity.

You can connect with me on:

🌐 https://www.ilovestellamaris.org

Made in the USA
Coppell, TX
01 August 2022

80765724R00036